BEFORE YOU STEP INTO THE OFFICE

How Focusing on Leadership Early
Can Set the Stage for Career Success

ROBERT YEO

Copyright © Robert Yeo, 2024

ISBN 978-1-915962-49-2
Published by Compass-Publishing UK

Cover artwork by © Dave Officer

Edited and designed by The Book Refinery Ltd
www.TheBookRefinery.com

All rights reserved. This book or any portion thereof may not be reproduced or used in any manner whatsoever without the express written permission of the publisher except for the use of brief quotations in a book review.

This book contains material designed to assist your business. While the author has made every effort to verify that the information provided in this book is correct and up to date, the author assumes no responsibility for any error, inaccuracy or omission.

The advice, examples and strategies contained herein are not suitable for every situation. The materials contained herein are not intended to represent or guarantee you will achieve your desired results, and the author shall not be liable for damages arising there from. Success is determined by a number of factors beyond the control of the author, including, but not limited to, market conditions, the capital on hand, effort levels and time.
You understand every individual business carries an inherent
risk of capital loss and failure.

For C&T

CONTENTS

Preface	7
Introduction	11
Leadership Toolkit	15
Principle #1 Grasp the Table Stakes	17
Principle #2 Invest in Yourself	20
Principle #3 Maintain Your Focus	23
Principle #4 Craft Your Unique Story	26
Principle #5 Cultivate Gravitas	29
Principle #6 Enhance Your Communication Skills	33
Principle #7 Be a Valued Team Member	37
Principle #8 Make Better Decisions	40
Principle #9 Engage Strategically with Stakeholders	44
Principle #10 Master Managing Upwards	46
Principle #11 Run Effective Meetings	50
Principle #12 Seek Out Feedback	53

All I Want To Know Is Where My Career Goes Off the Rails, so I'll Never Go There	57
Health Check: Personal Evaluation Tool (PET)	61
Conclusion	66
What's Next?	68
Reading, Watching and Listening List	70
About Me	72

PREFACE

A 2023 research article from Zenger Folkman[1] had me nodding in agreement. The notion? When it comes to leadership:

- ☑ it's easier to grasp when we're younger,
- ☑ an early start helps us sidestep detrimental habits, and
- ☑ the sooner we begin, the more time we have to refine our approach.

This Zenger Folkman research, which examined 17,000 leaders, highlights that only 10% of those people participated in their company's leadership development process in the first few years of their career.[2]

I've found that almost everyone I've worked with, me included, would have benefitted from starting on this leadership journey earlier in our professional lives.

This train of thought led me to ponder the upcoming professional foray of my two university-aged children. In the

---

[1] Zenger, J., 2019. *Leadership development: Are you starting too late?* Zenger Folkman [Online] https://www.zengerfolkman.com/wp-content/uploads/2019/08/LD-Are-You-Starting-Too-Late_WP-2019.pdf [Accessed 22 May 2023]
[2] Zenger, J., 2019. *Leadership development: Are you starting too late?* Zenger Folkman [Online] https://www.zengerfolkman.com/wp-content/uploads/2019/08/LD-Are-You-Starting-Too-Late_WP-2019.pdf [Accessed 22 May 2023]

next few years, they'll step into a professional world that will have been reshaped dramatically by shifts in business models, artificial intelligence (AI) and automation – a world that demands its future leaders innovate and adapt like never before.

At this point, I was reminded of the brilliant Seth Godin's avocado principles,[3] which suggest that waiting until you really need an avocado to buy one will be too late because the shops don't sell ripe ones. Therefore, it's necessary to anticipate your needs and prepare or act in advance, just as you'd need to buy an avocado before it's ripe if you plan to use it at its peak ripeness. Leadership and avocados – an intriguing connection. Who'd have thought they had something in common?

So, how can I contribute to this conversation sparked by Zenger Folkman's research on the belated commencement of leadership development? How can I make it resonate with my children and others who are about to join the workforce in a few short years?

Let's bring in an axiom of Reginald Revans, who was the founder of Action Learning:

> *For organisations to survive and grow, their rate of learning has to be equal to, or greater than, the rate of change in their environment. Learning > = Change.*

In my work as an executive coach, I've never seen this refuted in a meaningful way, so let's presume it to be true. Now let's refocus this axiom on the individual:

---

[3] Seth's Blog, 2019. *The avocado principles*. [Online] https://seths.blog/2019/04/the-avocado-principles/ [Accessed 5 June 2023]

For knowledge workers to differentiate and succeed, their rate of learning has to be equal to, or greater than, the rate of change in their environment.

Building upon Revans' axiom, we can develop the following propositions:

Proposition 1: Traditional education frequently falls short in teaching the necessary skills for career success. While schools and universities excel at teaching us to write notes, memorise facts and formulas, and solve technical problems, they frequently overlook the skills that are crucial for leadership success in collaborative environments, where sharing both knowledge and ideas is essential to driving innovation and growth.

Proposition 2: Leadership is universally accepted as essential and represents a growth industry. Consequently, individuals should be motivated to excel, which necessitates appropriate training. Practising leadership without proper training risks ingraining bad habits. The maxim "practice makes perfect" only holds if the practice is executed correctly. Emerging leaders are practising on the job, whether they're adequately trained or not.

Proposition 3: Leaders are made, not born. This implies that anyone can learn to be an effective leader with the right guidance and opportunities.

Proposition 4: Intelligence and technical competencies are necessary for success, but they aren't sufficient for leadership. Leadership is, in fact, behavioural. More specifically, the difference between leadership success and failure repeatedly comes down to behavioural skills such as communication, collaboration and prioritisation.

Proposition 5: Incentives are often misaligned. Organisations tend to focus on improvements that yield short-term gains, only spanning days, weeks, months or the next quarter. On the other hand, individuals stand to gain significantly from a longer-term horizon, as the skills they develop early on are compounded throughout their 20-, 30-, 40- or even 50-year careers.

Proposition 6: Leadership development starts too late. Early career education typically focuses on technical skills and compliance with policies and procedures. In contrast, leadership development programmes – frequently limited by cost constraints – are selective. These programmes are also prone to flawed selection processes that are influenced by past performance, visibility, politics and favouritism.

And so we arrive at this:

> *Leadership development should begin earlier, ideally before one's career even starts, to increase the odds of having a successful career. By being accountable and focusing on personal leadership development from the outset, individuals can better equip themselves for the challenges and opportunities that lie ahead in their professional lives.*

In the grand scheme of things, it's not merely about recognising the need for earlier leadership development but also about understanding the principles that anchor it. And the beauty of it is that these principles can be self-taught, self-improved and self-refined.

Drawing from my work coaching seasoned executives, I've curated a leadership toolkit to gift to my children and other interested individuals starting their careers.

INTRODUCTION

The why

Imagine diving headfirst into the deep end of the professional world, armed with a stack of leadership books and a pocketful of motivational quotes, only to discover that reality bears little resemblance to the neatly organised principles and step-by-step guides. As a flood of self-help advice on leadership renders it challenging to discern the signal from the noise, the disconnect between the idealised world of management theories and the chaotic, fast-paced reality of the modern workplace worsens. This is a reality where the following is true:

- Following your passion is terrible advice that already successful people tell young people. To paraphrase Professor Scott Galloway:

    The billionaires invited to speak at business schools to give the follow your passion *advice don't have amazing insights into life and careers. Your job is something you're good at, and then you spend thousands of hours getting better – through grit, perseverance and the sacrifice required to break through hard things to excel at it. The problem with following your passion is that work is hard. When you run into obstacles and face injustices, a common guaranteed attribute*

> *of the workplace, you'll start thinking, "I'm not loving this. It's upsetting and hard. It must not be my passion." This is a poor litmus test. Most people, early in their careers, should pursue their passions on weekends.*

- The typical graduate training programme will do a good job of providing minimal training to keep you safe, make you entry-level productive, and protect the employer by ensuring you follow workplace policies and procedures.
- The average established leader is understandably so wrapped up in trying to comprehend, cope with and create value at their own level that they have little time to get involved with the complexities of projects down the food chain. So, instead of helping more-junior people to adapt to and develop the leadership skills for working in complexity, many simply bark orders to manage the work.
- The returns for top talent in all spheres of life have never been higher. A small percentage of professionals obtain disproportionate recognition and, usually, a high percentage of the spoils available.

Today's graduates face unprecedented challenges in a landscape transformed by rapid changes to business models, AI and automation. The next generation of leaders must adapt and innovate as never before, learning from the past and from others, while forging their own path through the messy, unpredictable world that awaits them.

What would it look like if you collected lists of techniques for doing fantastic work early in your career? I decided to find out by using the knowledge I've gained from coaching successful executives for the past decade. Partly, my goal was to create a guide that could be used by young adults who will soon start their careers, but I was also curious about distilling the common themes from my work with experienced executives and presenting it so people just starting out can also benefit. One thing that jumps out is that it's not just advice saying, "Work harder."

Each of the 12 principles I advance has needed to pass these three filters:

1. I believe in them because I've done this in my past career or I've helped my clients do it.

2. They're practical and actionable, and it doesn't take much effort to start implementing them.

3. They help you to have a career in which AI can't readily imitate you.

Who's this book for?

The following toolkit assumes you're very ambitious and curious to understand what building blocks are essential to having a successful career.

It also assumes you're a knowledge worker. A knowledge worker leverages technologies, data and interdisciplinary knowledge to innovate, solve complex problems and create value in the digital age. A knowledge worker is typically characterised by continuous learning, technological proficiency, collaboration and teamwork, adaptability, value creation, and broader, global perspectives. They not only "think for a living" but can also navigate a complex, interconnected and rapidly changing landscape.

How to get the most from this book

At any one time, people of equal intelligence and skill can produce unequal results due to small differences. The 12 principles provide the steps that make a difference for the ambitious, early career knowledge worker.

Read the principles and put them into practice. For each of the principles, create new ideas, alternative solutions and hypotheses that you can experiment with in low-risk ways to see what works for you. Iterate. Make small, incremental changes, which will become permanent changes to your behaviour, skills and capabilities. These small changes will compound during your career, steering you to leadership and career success.

When you've finished reading this book, use the personal evaluation tool (PET) on page 61. What insights have you gained? Your answers will help to clarify, define and prioritise the areas to work on.

Commonly, people will be juggling too many priorities, often competing to find enough time to think and reflect. Yet because our memories are selective, we tend to focus on the positives, so it's easy to forget the actual lessons. At the end of each week, review and reflect on what's working and what isn't. Repeat the PET self-assessment exercise when you feel in need of guidance and to cut through the clutter that will build up around you at work.

LEADERSHIP TOOLKIT

I created a leadership toolkit for your first job so you'll avoid forming bad habits and feeling lost when challenges arise. Here are 12 practical tips I wish I'd known sooner that will kick-start your leadership journey. The principles I advance don't just represent my personal opinions; they're the quintessence of what I've learned from coaching successful executives.

Principle #1. Grasp the table stakes: Deliver on spec, on time and on budget. Consistency, even in small actions, is key. Leave strategy to others initially.

Principle #2. Invest in yourself: Say *yes* early in your career. View spending time and money on learning, tools and new habits as fuel for success.

Principle #3. Maintain focus: Avoid distractions. Staying focused on top priorities sets successful people apart.

Principle #4. Craft your unique story: Understand and control your personal brand. Know what words people associate with you.

Principle #5. Cultivate gravitas: Develop your presence. Gravitas can lead others to feel more confident in you, irrespective of your experience.

Principle #6. Enhance your communication skills: Effective communication is key. Master listening, writing and public speaking.

Principle #7. Be a valued team member: Aim to be a collaborator, not just a leader. Working with others to achieve goals is vital early in your career.

Principle #8. Make better decisions: Use robust frameworks for decision-making. Recognise the trade-offs involved.

Principle #9. Engage strategically with stakeholders: Networking isn't self-promotion; it's essential. Build relationships strategically.

Principle #10. Master managing upwards: Communicate proactively to show control. Managing your manager shows initiative and empowerment.

Principle #11. Run effective meetings: Your well-run meetings can stand out amid poorly managed ones. Free up headspace and time for others.

Principle #12. Seek out feedback: Maintain a feedback loop for continuous improvement, like elite sports teams do.

Principle #1

GRASP THE TABLE STAKES

"But that's your job. That's what you're being paid to do."

The coaching session is a private, confidential space carved away from the hectic nature of my clients' day-to-day jobs and line management. Therefore, it's no surprise when clients choose this haven to unburden themselves, as if undergoing a cathartic ritual. Often, they lack faith in those around them or above them, hesitating to share their thoughts and perspectives on a myriad of subjects.

A pivotal role in my coaching practice is to challenge and keep them answerable. Thus, I find it not only suitable but necessary to point out the seemingly self-evident:

"You're the leader!"

"If you aren't going to do it, who is?"

The responsibility falls squarely on your shoulders, whether it be managing workplace disputes, addressing an underperforming supplier, dealing with a less committed team member, rectifying errors or providing clear directives during a crisis.

Those who don't get this will rarely last very long in the role or will end up doing the low-value, tedious work that the most talented people don't want to spend their time on.

In the early stages of your career, *it's your job* to complete tasks and generate more value than you cost.

You aren't the "strategy person".

Yet.

To be a big-picture thinker, you must first earn the respect, trust and credibility of the people around you. The only way you can do this is through delivering tangible value – *consistently*.

> **TRIP HAZARD**
>
> You allow the pursuit of perfection to get in the way of the work you need to do. Perfectionism is often a place in which to hide. Perfection can be an excuse we use not to speak up or deliver.

Focus on bringing results to your day job, not laying out frameworks, plans or blue-sky thinking. Leave the strategy to others in the first few years of your career.

The "table stakes" in business are the minimum offering it takes to be considered a player in the market. The way for you to start differentiating is through executing. These are your table stakes!

Here's another way to think about it: act with integrity in everything you do from day one on the job. But what does that mean? Everyone likely has a different definition of integrity. To me, integrity means this:

- Doing what I say I'll do when I say I'll do it, and doing it in the expected way.
- And if I can't get it done, I'll be responsible for that mess and clean it up.

Consistency, **integrity** and holding yourself **accountable** for delivering "on spec, on time and on budget", while not flashy marketing buzzwords, are three words highly correlated to success at work.

Before you know it, your managers will trust you more because your actions align with your commitments, and you consistently do what you say you'll do. You'll establish credibility and hence be credible to more senior people – and your opinion on broader topics will now be welcome.

You now can be the "strategy person".

> **Do you do what you say you'll do when you say you'll do it?**

Principle #2

INVEST IN YOURSELF

My clients are busy, driven people. Many are senior executives who are regarded as successful, having made it to the most senior levels of their profession: partners, managing directors and C-suite executives. The most successful ones invest in continuous learning throughout their careers and don't rely upon their employers and superiors to direct it. They operate from a "growth and abundance" mindset, which acts as an accelerator for their careers. They don't allow their skills and knowledge to lose value steadily. They invest in themselves.

Learning continuously can be expensive in terms of time and effort, but standing still and not furthering one's personal development costs a fortune.

Warren Buffet, the CEO of Berkshire Hathaway, sums it up perfectly:

> *Generally speaking, investing in yourself is the best thing you can do. Anything that improves your own talents – nobody can tax it or take it away from you.*

You could have made the best decision in the history of good decision-making in taking this role, joining the company and becoming a team member. Yet if you don't invest in yourself, you're effectively multiplying by zero.

So what should you focus on when investing in yourself?

First, at the start of your career, your top priority is to invest in the technical skills and competencies relevant to your day job. Excelling at your day job is your top priority. Set yourself the brief of becoming the *best-informed person* in your team on the tasks, projects and areas you're assigned. Learn all about your clients, technologies, tools and projects, and the ins and outs of the business. Many people you'll work with are too lazy to do this kind of homework.

Second, spend your twenties saying *yes* and the rest of your life saying *no*. In your twenties, early in your career, say yes to everything. It expands your luck surface area (the chance of good things happening for you) and lets you explore further. Later in your career, it will be the time to say no to almost everything.

In the initial stage of your career, saying yes and building a reputation for figuring things out is a clear way to stand out.

Saying yes gets you into the rooms and conversations you need to be in.

Another way of thinking about this is to *work hard and then work smart*. If you prefer to spend all your spare time doing other (non-work) things, I may like you better, but then don't complain you aren't being promoted fast enough.

Third, learn to write better. Writing about something, even something you know well (or think you do) usually shows you that you didn't know it as well as you thought. Writing about something teaches you what you know, what you don't know and how to think. Writing about something is one of the best ways to learn about it. Writing isn't just a vehicle to share ideas with others but is also a way to understand them better yourself. Writing isn't going away in the world of AI and automation. In fact, clear thinking and writing will grow in importance as the broader noise level increases exponentially.

> **TRIP HAZARD**
>
> You don't look after yourself: you're lacking sleep, exercise, rest, good food and time to recharge. If you don't make time for your wellness, you'll be forced to make time for your illness.

Last, but certainly not least, is investing time and energy into improving your so-called "soft skills". Soft skills should really be called "**smart skills**". It's vital to master these skills as your career develops, because leadership is behavioural. Leadership success or failure doesn't just happen; the difference between the two generally comes down to our personal behaviours, so it makes sense to start early on your path to mastering these skills – which are ones such as collaboration, communication, negotiation, creative thinking, deep focus and empathy. *Soft skills are smart skills.*

> Are you investing in yourself and creating an edge, or are you moving with the tide, comfortable doing the same thing everyone else does?

Principle #3

MAINTAIN YOUR FOCUS

What things do you wish you'd said no to recently?

I say no a lot, and here's why.

I want to be world-class at one thing: to be an executive coach and trusted partner who helps people make a bigger impact and strive for answers to create the changes they need to be able to succeed.

With that goal in mind, I regularly exercise the skill of saying no to ensure I remain focused and cut out distractions. Each no is aligned with my aim to help my clients turn conversations about possibilities and strategies into tangible actions and results.

The most successful people I coach are experts at saying no to keep their top priorities front and centre. This contrasts sharply with a trap many people fall into: they have, over time, become unfocused, which often leads to a sense of stuckness. These are some common symptoms of being unfocused:

- A packed calendar with no room to breathe.
- Neglecting essential parts of your life, such as family, relationships and health.
- Underinvestment in self-development.

Being unfocused is one of the common chronic issues I see with my clients when they start working with me. They struggle to explain their priorities concisely and clearly without resorting to a lengthy list of to-dos. One of my recent clients serves as a cautionary tale. A diligent corporate citizen, this person always said yes to tasks and projects. Despite their hard work, they kept missing out on promotions, and their earnings had plateaued. They'd diluted their impact and spread themselves across too many responsibilities. It's common for successful executives to become distracted. Everyone wants a piece of them, and they frequently become magnets that attract all kinds of extras.

> **TRIP HAZARD**
>
> You forget why you're in business. Who are your clients, and what do they want? And how does your work and your team's work support that?

Although it's advisable to embrace opportunities early in your career – as principle #2 suggests, saying *yes* to everything can increase your chances of positive outcomes – there's a risk of becoming unfocused and losing sight of your core responsibilities. Remember the reasons behind your role: understand your clients' needs, recognise how your work and that of your team add value, and remain steadfast in your business objectives.

The key to success lies in avoiding distractions and maintaining focus on your top priorities. Successful individuals distinguish themselves by eliminating irrelevant distractions, ensuring they don't squander time and energy on trivial matters.

Adopt a mindset in which your top priority is viewed as the "oxygen" that's essential for your team's or business's survival. While numerous demands will always vie for your attention, they mustn't overshadow this vital priority. Without it, a business is as doomed as a human without air. Other seemingly high priorities are the food and drink, not the oxygen, for a business. You can last for days without water or weeks without food.

What's your oxygen?

Principle #4

CRAFT YOUR UNIQUE STORY

For years, I've been coaching leaders who are often on top of their game but find themselves tripping over one common obstacle: **self-awareness**.

A lack of self-awareness can be risky at best and disastrous at worst.

The term "self-awareness" can be as elusive as it is ubiquitous, but I like Dr Tasha Eurich's definition in her book *Insight*.[4] She describes self-awareness as this:

> *The ability to see ourselves clearly – understand who we are, how others see us, and how we fit into the world around us.*

Self-awareness isn't one truth. It's a complex tapestry woven from various threads of information.

In my coaching practice, a recurring theme is helping clients manage or engage with individuals suffering from low self-

---

4. Eurich, T., 2018. *Insight*. London: Pan Macmillan.

awareness, which negatively affects those around them. These individuals habitually misinterpret constructive criticism as a personal affront, responding with volatile outbursts directed at their team, their peers and even their manager. They mistakenly draw the wrong lessons from good outcomes. They think their abrasive, erratic, egotistical approach drives high team performance. Whereas the team's success will often be despite those behaviours. If asked, they don't need to change. Everyone else is the problem.

Eventually, their bad behaviour catches up with them, with the inevitable consequences for their career. Because they haven't built relationships and engendered trust, they find any alliances are illusionary – leaving them unsupported when they need it most.

So, how can you ensure you're not setting yourself up for this kind of failure? Start cultivating self-awareness early in your career. To initiate this process, ask yourself this: "What three words would my closest colleagues use to describe me?" This question is the beginning of sculpting your personal brand – a brand that's more than just a label; it's an asset.

Your brand has intrinsic value. It fosters recognition, influences perceptions, builds trust and heightens confidence. Being more than just an abstract concept, your personal brand offers tangible dividends, which contribute to your future career's net present value.

Consider the most successful companies: their brands shape public perception, from reputation and customer service to innovation and environmental impact. A robust brand not only enhances a company's value by attracting and retaining customers but it also guides and motivates employees, conveying the company's story and mission. Your personal brand functions similarly. It's crucial to recognise that your brand exists, whether actively cultivated or not.

> **TRIP HAZARD**
>
> You over-focus on your personal brand, and your brand and craft become divorced. Investing in your brand takes precedence over investing in getting better at your craft.

If you let others dictate your narrative, their assumptions and perceptions become your brand. Reflect on this question: "What do people think of when they hear my name?" If you're uncertain, seek insights from your peers or revisit past feedback from projects, courses or performance reviews. These perceptions form the foundation of your current brand.

Now reframe the question: "What do I *want* people to think of when they hear my name?" This is your chance to craft your unique story. Think carefully about your desired brand values. They should align with who you are, what you stand for and your actions, so that they'll become an effective toolkit for helping to expand your influence and impact.

> What do you want people to think of when they hear your name?

Principle #5

CULTIVATE GRAVITAS

Have you ever encountered someone who you'd describe as a "force"? There's a power to them that you want to join. You'll notice a lot of things: their confidence, their dignity and that the space around them feels different when you enter it. They emanate a kind of magnetic pull that captures the attention of everyone in the room.

So, what's their secret?

One word: **gravitas**.

The impact of gravitas could not be more profound, and it extends far beyond mere charisma. And the best part? It doesn't have to start at the top. Gravitas can start with you.

But what exactly is gravitas? Why is it so important, and how can you cultivate it?

Gravitas is often linked with perceptions of influence, authority, dignity and importance. The power of this perception is so compelling that it can inspire confidence in others, regardless of their initial judgement based on experience, education or skills. In essence, gravitas has the ability to eclipse and dominate other attributes. Moreover, it's something that can be nurtured from the very beginning of your career.

In today's ever-competitive business landscape, gravitas stands as one of the most crucial attributes for career development. Possessing gravitas can significantly enhance your professional trajectory, particularly for those aiming for leadership roles and top-tier positions.

In my work as an executive coach, I've guided clients in cultivating the foundational elements that make up gravitas. They've found that mastering gravitas isn't just a personal advantage; rather, it's a competitive edge in attracting and retaining top talent. Gravitas draws people in, compelling them to want to work with you and to be part of your team. On the flip side, an underdeveloped sense of gravitas usually manifests as low energy levels, heightened anxiety, and an overly casual demeanour in both body language and appearance. Remember, perceptions matter, especially in business. In a world of fleeting encounters, first impressions can leave an indelible mark and may represent missed opportunities to advocate for your team and your ideas.

> **TRIP HAZARD**
>
> You chase prestige. It's okay to want to impress other people, but choose the right people. At best, prestige is a trailing indicator. At worst, it increases the noise level and hence increases distraction.

So who has left an impression on you throughout your education and career? Was it a teacher, an educator, or someone renowned in the business or entertainment sectors? Or perhaps a politician whose impact has been lasting? Take a moment to reflect on those individuals who, for you, embody the essence of gravitas.

Chances are that these people have demonstrated some or all of the following elements:

Key Ways To Demonstrate Gravitas	< Low	High >
Confident without being arrogant		
Lacks anxiety, even under pressure		
Purposeful and passionate; inspires others to achieve their best.		
Has good judgement and is prepared to make decisions and not be indecisive.		
Commands respect and is respectful		
A clear and powerful communicator.		
Makes impactful and lasting impressions and takes care regarding appearance and body language.		
Acts with integrity, doing what they say they'll do, when they say they'll do it and in the expected way.		

On each of the eight rows in the table, place an X where you see yourself today on the scale from Low to High. Next, place an O where you'd like to be in 6–12 months' time. Be transparently honest with yourself when placing the X and O; your answers will help you to define and prioritise your goals and desired outcomes.

Select no more than three gravitas elements from the previous table to work on. What small experiments could you do to shift yourself from where you are currently to where you want to be?

> **Who has left a lasting impression on you throughout your education or career?**

Principle #6

ENHANCE YOUR COMMUNICATION SKILLS

Effective communication lies at the heart of both a business's strengths and its weaknesses. When problems arise and employees become upset, the overarching complaint is often about the need for better communication.

But what exactly does "better communication" entail?

Danny Meyer, in his book *Setting the Table,*[5] boils it down to this:

> *Understanding **who** needs to know **what**.*
> ***When** people need to know it and **why**.*
> *And then presenting the information in an entirely comprehensive **way**.*

In my experience of conducting 360-degree-feedback reviews and coaching interviews, it's rare for executives to receive high praise for the frequency *and* content of their communication. The root cause? Employees have a voracious appetite for understanding what's happening in the business. Exceptional

---

5. Meyer, D., 2010. *Setting the Table*. London: Marshall Cavendish International.

leaders communicate both formally and informally. They're transparent and candid, ensuring that team members not only understand their own status but also the overall state, direction and rationale of the business.

This principle also applies to executives who become frustrated with a team member's actions – or lack thereof. When such issues inevitably crop up in coaching sessions, I frequently challenge these executives by asking, "Is your frustration stemming from standards you failed to communicate?" This question usually prompts a moment of reflection followed by a wry smile or a nod, acknowledging their own role in the communication breakdown.

Clear, concise and timely communication often represents low-hanging fruit: it's easily identifiable and swiftly addressed. Yet, I've observed numerous hardworking, competent professionals struggling to make their desired impact due to mediocre communication skills. Surprisingly, few actively seek to improve this critical area, despite it being one of the simplest ways to boost influence and impact.

The most common forum for speaking in front of peers and bosses is the all-too-familiar meeting – a staple of the modern workplace. Whether these meetings occur in person or over platforms such as Zoom/Teams, they offer prime opportunities to stand out through active participation and making impactful contributions.

In meetings, whether they're face-to-face or virtual, ask yourself this: How did you prepare? What's your posture like? Are you fully engaged, or are you distracted by messages? Are you putting more energy into the room than you're taking out?

Here are six strategies I see top performers using to make their communication more impactful:

1. **Practice:** They seize every chance to speak in public, using opportunities such as graduate recruitment, volunteer work and training sessions to hone their skills in lower-pressure environments.

2. **Preparation:** They never enter meetings unprepared. They research the agenda, formulate opinions and consider alternative perspectives in advance.

> **TRIP HAZARD**
>
> You become a fast-talking, assertive speaker as a way of pushing your agenda past other people's examination. This is at the expense of developing your listening skills as you emphasise listening to respond rather than to gain understanding.

3. **Body language:** They know that perceptions and inferences formed are often the result of body language and non-verbal cues. They pay attention to their posture, hand movements, eye contact, attire and even their background in virtual meetings.

4. **Personal stories:** They employ evocative, personal narratives to enliven their presentations and arguments. Stories resonate with us all and make messages more memorable.

5. **Audience awareness:** They invest time in understanding their audience and meeting participants. Knowing who will be in the room, their potential viewpoints and preparing for questions ensures they're rarely caught off guard.

6. **Listen, question and speak assertively:** They listen respectfully, ask clarifying questions to understand different points of view, and speak assertively with minimal waffle and no BS. They'll acknowledge if they don't know the answer to a question – and they'll take ownership of following up with the pertinent information.

Employing these strategies increases the chance of meetings having high energy levels – with lots of participation and ideas flowing freely, whether or not everyone agrees with the outcome. This type of meeting is analogous to an exothermic chemical reaction in which energy is released as reactants are combined and the energy becomes available for use.

- Exothermic reaction: reactants → products + energy
- Exothermic meeting: people → ideas + energy

The alternative is an endothermic meeting in which people rarely engage, don't volunteer their thoughts, and don't put forward suggestions and ideas. Participants not contributing makes it feel like they're removing energy from the room.

- Endothermic reaction: reactants → products – energy
- Endothermic meeting: people → ideas – energy

> **Are you putting more energy into the room than you're taking out?**

Principle #7

BE A VALUED TEAM MEMBER

I want to share an important truth that very few people agree with me on; that is, something I believe that most people don't.

To paraphrase the author Gordon Curphy:

> *All organisations want collaboration and teamwork, yet they do just about everything possible to ensure it doesn't happen! Between matrix reporting lines, frequent job rotations, leaders not getting any training on how to build teams or feedback on team dynamics and performance, and rewards systems incentivising individual accomplishments over collective ones, there should be little wonder that only a small minority of teams are high-performing ones.*[6]

Organisations have a lot more to do before they become team-friendly by default.

What does this mean for someone who has only recently started their career journey?

---

[6] Curphy, D. [Comment] in Dole, J. 2023. *Are you rethinking 2024 performance management as you plan for 2023 end of year reviews?* [Post] LinkedIn. https://www.linkedin.com/posts/jdole_team-based-performance-management-strategies-activity-7112427476869373952-QoAp?utm_source=share&utm_medium=member_desktop [Accessed 5 October 2023]

In an organisational setting, almost all work is conducted in teams. To be successful, organisations need to have teams that work together and in which individuals align their interests and put aside differences to focus individually and collectively on what's best for the organisation. Teamwork doesn't happen naturally among groups of people, especially those containing driven high performers. You need someone playing the role of the team's coach to make it happen. That's the team leader.

At the earlier stages of your career, you'll work for the team leader and be a team member. Therefore, your job is to become a valued team member and to collaborate effectively with the rest of the team.

High-performing teams share a number of attributes:

1. The team members have a shared view of the situation surrounding the team, especially who their crucial stakeholders are and the characteristics of the broader environment, such as competition and the market and economic factors impacting them.
2. They're committed to a common purpose. They understand why the team exists and what success looks like.
3. There are clear rules of engagement for the team, such as team member norms, which help achieve team cohesion.
4. They demonstrate a "team-first, not me-first" attitude and are committed to accomplishing the assigned tasks.
5. High-performing teams stay focused. They measure results against team goals, track progress regularly, and learn collectively from successes and failures.

6. Team members are comfortable owning up to mistakes, challenging each other and holding each other accountable for the team's common goals.

Many team leaders don't know how to develop and run teams because they've never been trained to do so. They do well in their day jobs, so additional responsibilities – including managing people – come their way. There's an assumption that new managers will work out what needs to be done because they've shown themselves to be successful in their responsibilities so far.

> **TRIP HAZARD**
>
> You think of the for-profit company you work for as a family, rather than as a sports team that only exists to provide a top-quality product or service to its clients.

Early in your career, you can help them by being available and flexible, asking for clarification if things are unclear, and focusing on doing your best work and getting on with your fellow team members as much as possible. Later in your career, you can build and develop your own high-performing team. But for now, aim to be your team's best, most valuable member.

> How focused are you on your own goals versus the team's?

Principle #8

MAKE BETTER DECISIONS

A core principle of effective leadership is making decisions, and the more senior you get, the more you must get used to making decisions based on incomplete and imperfect information.

Navigating decisions under such constraints isn't just a useful skill; it's an imperative. In today's fast-paced, intricate business landscape, waiting for every piece of the puzzle before making a move isn't just impractical – it's detrimental. The pitfalls of analysis paralysis are many: deferred decisions often resurface at the least opportune moments, forcing leaders into choices that are anything but optimal.

Given my line of work, it's hardly a revelation that I frequently coach clients on honing their decision-making prowess. Whether it's pushing them beyond their comfort zones to explore unconventional solutions or introducing structured frameworks to mitigate cognitive biases, the goal remains the same: *better decisions*.

Cognitive biases are at work whenever we make decisions. A cognitive bias is a systematic error in thinking that occurs when we process and interpret information in the world around us. It affects the decisions and judgements we make. Frameworks such as performing a project premortem[7] or using Chesterton's fence[8] will help identify problems earlier so you can address them proactively before they become more significant.

Not all decisions are equal. Therefore, using a heuristic to facilitate problem-solving and decision-making can be helpful:

- Is this situation – a problem or opportunity – significant enough to require a robust framework and additional information and perspectives? These are "Type 1" decisions.
- Is my informed intuition, judgement and experience sufficient to make the decision quickly? These are "Type 2" decisions.

The following describes these two types of decision in more detail.

Type 1 decisions – consequential and irreversible

For Type 1 decisions, which are those that are more consequential and irreversible, the emphasis should be shifted to processes that elevate decision quality. Robust decision-making frameworks, sources of feedback and diverse points of view are all essential for reducing the risk of making poor decisions.

---

[7] Klein, G., 2007. Performing a project premortem. *Harvard Business Review*, September 2007. [Online] https://hbr.org/2007/09/performing-a-project-premortem/ [Accessed 26 June 2023]

[8] Farnam Street. *Chesterton's Fence: A lesson in second order thinking*. [Online] https://fs.blog/chestertons-fence/ [Accessed 26 June 2023]

These are decisions that have the potential to change the trajectory of our careers.

Think of these as Decisions, with a big "D". Once made, they're usually fixed and inflexible.

The most successful executives I coach employ frameworks to improve the quality of their decisions and mitigate cognitive biases for these Type 1 decisions. Frameworks help them avoid common issues such as groupthink, self-interest, and confirmation

> **TRIP HAZARD**
>
> You gain early success and traction because you're ambitious and talented. Beware! Early success can make you overconfident, which will cause you to ignore or forget these core principles. This creates blind spots, and blind spots may derail your career.

and anchoring bias. We're all guilty of having these cognitive biases. If un-mitigated, they'll inevitably lead to poor decisions. Nearly everyone would benefit from learning about cognitive biases. The best summary I have discovered is by Marcus Lu,[9] which I recommend you print out and bookmark.

Type 2 decisions – inconsequential and reversible

Contrast the Type 1 decisions with decisions of lesser consequence and that are reversible. You don't have to live with the results. You can change your mind relatively quickly and

---

9. Lu, M., 2020. *50 Cognitive biases in the modern world*. Visual Capitalist. [Online] https://visualcapitalist.com/50-cognitive-biases-in-the-modern-world/ [Accessed 10 December 2022]

with little impact if the original outcome isn't quite what you want.

These are decisions with a small "d". There's little impact on your life if the original outcome differs from what you want.

The pitfall many busy executives face is allocating too much time and energy to this type of decision. These are small decisions that should be made quickly, with the available information, or even delegated to others. Successful executives develop habits that help them to sidestep overthinking and procrastination.

Decisions come in all shapes and sizes. Early in your career, when you have the opportunity to influence decisions around you, you should take it rather than sit back and allow someone else to. The key lies in stacking the odds in your favour before deciding. To do so, you first need to know what type of decision you're facing. Is it Type 1 or Type 2?

Where are you focusing your mental resources to make the most-effective decisions?

Principle #9
ENGAGE STRATEGICALLY WITH STAKEHOLDERS

In any organisational setting, work predominantly operates through relationships – be they with team members, peers or clients.

The most adept leaders I encounter excel by harnessing their "network intelligence". When faced with challenges, they have the ability to draw upon a wealth of ideas and expertise beyond their immediate circle.

Here are seven motivations for building strong relationships:

1. **Learn how best to work with your boss:** This is perhaps the most crucial of relationships at work.

2. **Understand your fellow team members and build trust:** You'll thereby be accomplishing more than a group of individuals would.

3. **Help solve real business problems:** Your network will know things you don't know; they can help stress test your ideas and reduce the risk of repeating mistakes others have previously made.

4. **Identify a sponsor:** This should be someone more senior than you and who will have your back in those important career conversations that happen when you aren't in the room.

5. **Find a mentor:** This should be someone more experienced than you and outside your line management. They'll be the person to go to for advice on what to try next.

6. **Expand your luck surface area:** Creating a diverse network increases your chances of stumbling upon new opportunities and avoiding potential setbacks.

7. **Find your next job:** The best job opportunities often come from your second- and third-degree connections.

A common pitfall many junior professionals make is to neglect building relationships, which I find puzzling.

What are you so busy doing that you don't have the time, energy or capacity to build relationships?

Allocate and protect time for meeting new people, re-engaging with old contacts and deepening existing relationships. Doing this is as close to a sure thing as possible. It's a no-brainer. Replace the term "networking" with "relationship building". While the former feels like a task to tick off, the latter represents a lasting opportunity for growth and learning.

> **TRIP HAZARD**
>
> You surround yourself with people who drain your energy rather than those who energise you, or with those who are B or C players, rather than A players, which drags you down.

> What are you so busy doing that you don't have the time, energy or capacity to build relationships?

Principle #10
MASTER MANAGING UPWARDS

One thing I've observed is that the most successful people I work with see their relationships with their bosses very differently.

They aren't trying to avoid the person. They may not always agree, but they engage with them constructively. And as a minimum, they know where they stand.

They see the relationship as crucial to their success, and they manage it intentionally, knowing they're bound by a common purpose and must interact positively.

First of all, and I say this from experience as someone who's had 16 managers during my professional and financial services career, it's important to set realistic expectations for your boss. I don't say this in bad faith but because their time and energy aren't infinite. Leaders at higher levels are often so focused on their own challenges that they may not have ample time to delve into the weeds of tasks and projects further down the organisational chart. Of course, you might get lucky. Of the many managers I've had, half were genuinely interested in guiding me proactively. At the same time, a smaller number were open to feedback and willing to adapt their own way of thinking and operating.

What distinguishes the most successful people is their skill in "managing up". They communicate proactively to show they're in control, thereby reducing unnecessary and inefficient back-and-forth or endless one-off questions.

> **TRIP HAZARD**
>
> You endure, without attempting to improve the situation, the realities of working for a manager who doesn't want to engage or develop their direct reports.

They take the initiative and empower themselves in several ways, as described in the following hierarchy (starting at #1):[10]

1. They rarely wait to be told what to do.
2. They ask for permission judiciously.
3. They aren't shy about making recommendations.
4. They often lead with phrases such as "I intend to..."
5. They take action and report back immediately.
6. They take action and report back periodically.
7. They take action and simply report back upon completion.

This capability to provide the right amount of information and context is invaluable. It not only assists their boss but also fosters a sense of trust and confidence, leading to increased empowerment and autonomy.

---

[10] Covey, S., 2004. *The 8th Habit*. London: Simon & Schuster UK Ltd.

Effective followers of a leader are mission-focused, driven to win, not afraid to tell their bosses what is and is not working, and seek forgiveness rather than ask permission. With that in mind, let's look at what you're working on. For each initiative, project or task you're investing your time and attention in, run it past the seven previous steps and decide which is the most accurate for your current way of working and interacting with your boss:

1. Did you get handed the task and were told to "just get it done" or were asked "please look into this"?

2. Did you ask your boss whether it was okay for you to spend time on that problem or opportunity?

3. Did you recommend that "we deal with this issue" or "we seize the opportunity"?

4. In your latest one-to-one with your boss, did you tell them, "I intend to spend time on X"?

5. After addressing a new issue, did you immediately inform your boss that you had done X to fix Y?

6. Do you give regular updates to your boss on a fluid set of initiatives you are focused on, some at the start, some during and some at the end of each project?

7. In your regular catch-ups, did you let your boss know that you had completed the review and then concluded that the solution is now being implemented for a problem your boss wasn't even aware of?

What level of initiative are you most commonly working at?

A final point, as there's an important distinction to make: managing up to curry favours and position yourself for promotion is all too common in the workplace; however, managing upwards to help your team accomplish its goals is preferred. People who are effective at getting promoted are significantly different to work with compared to those who are effective at teamwork and developing their teams.

What level of initiative do you feel comfortable operating at?

Principle #11

RUN EFFECTIVE MEETINGS

There's a common premise held by the highest performers I work with: time is your most valuable asset, so don't waste time and energy on things that don't matter.

The desire to not waste time is laced throughout everything high performers do, and it particularly impacts their internal meeting attendance and how they run meetings themselves. They ask, "Is a meeting required?"; "Should I attend?"; and "What value will it add?"

Decision fatigue is real. With finite cognitive bandwidth, every distraction and superfluous meeting chips away at our ability to make high-impact choices. High performers are acutely aware of this, and they strive to protect and prioritise their mental energy judiciously.

The troubling trend over the past decades is that the notion of "doing work" has increasingly been conflated with "attending meetings". As a general rule, most meetings – whether in person or via Zoom/Teams – are a waste of time. Why? Because most are poorly run and don't achieve the desired results, or the existence of the meeting is a symptom of earlier poor communication.

People starting their careers don't all say, "I want to do the same thing everyone else is doing," and yet, there's a comfort in surrounding yourself with people doing the same thing you're doing by attending meeting after meeting.

Unlike the average worker, high performers exercise a degree of control over their schedules. Akin to elite athletes who manage their training regimens meticulously, high-performing business people control their work schedules. They know that thinking a full schedule is a proxy for their seriousness is a trap, and it's one they're keen to avoid.

TRIP HAZARD

You encounter people who don't want to change, which leads to frustration and resentment. Change is hard. Every change carries with it the possibility of conflict and uncertainty. Your boss, who leads many of the meetings you attend, may regard the workplace environment as dynamic and difficult enough without looking for trouble.

To pull away from the traps that most fall into, here are six things I see top performers doing when they run meetings, which you should try out as soon as possible:

1. They have a desired outcome and have taken the time to understand the incentives and motivation of the key players, so as to frame the conversation and engage them fully.
2. They start and finish on time; finishing early is even better.

3. The attendees understand the meeting's purpose and their role as a participant.
4. They always send a well-defined agenda at least a day in advance, which includes updates on previously agreed actions and allows for additional items to be added.
5. The agenda is prioritised, and each item is assigned an owner and a clear objective: is it to update the group, is it to pass on important information or is a decision required?
6. They allocate time to recap at the end of every meeting to clarify commitments. They ask the group, "What have we decided today?" Then, the decisions and actions are summarised, and the owners take them away.

Many managers struggle with meeting efficacy, often replicating the flawed approaches they've experienced. As someone early in your career, you can be a positive influence. Even as a participant, you can offer to contribute to the agenda or circulate a post-meeting summary, thereby supporting your manager and subtly introducing better practices.

How do you rate the meetings you attend?

Principle #12

SEEK OUT FEEDBACK

"I'm curious. How did they respond when you gave them this feedback?"

Cue the tumbleweed as the silence grows.

When problems arise and people become upset and complain about their teammates, boss or other workplace colleagues, the underlying reason is often a lack of feedback. Many people are simply unaware of their shortcomings, residing in a state of "unconscious incompetence". They need help getting better. To shift from this state to become "consciously competent", they need clear, actionable feedback. (Both of these states are in reference to the four stages of competence, aka the Conscious Competence Ladder, attributed to Noel Burch of Gordon Training International, which was developed in the 1970s.)

Without feedback, they won't know what to start doing or stop doing. It's invaluable. However, helpful feedback rarely originates from a sanitised annual performance review. Instead, it's from the observations and advice that are all of the following:

- Timely
- Relevant
- Constructive
- Actionable

Despite claims of fostering a "feedback culture", many organisations – especially those in the professional and financial services sectors – fall short. The feedback they offer tends to be diluted and often relegated to annual bonuses or performance reviews that are neither timely nor specific.

A prevailing notion among the high performers I coach is that you must seek out different perspectives to be smarter and stronger. The challenge is that the more you ascend the corporate hierarchy, the less likely you are to receive candid feedback. Fewer individuals are willing to share frank opinions about your decisions and leadership style. This predicament, which is sometimes dubbed the "CEO disease", can be a hindrance. Hence, it's in our interest to pursue feedback proactively, thus facilitating intellectual and professional growth.

> **TRIP HAZARD**
>
> You become dissatisfied because you compare yourself to others. As you get more years under your belt, you'll come across many successful people who didn't deserve the credit they got. It doesn't matter. Play your game and focus on yourself. Comparison is the thief of joy.

Many busy, driven people frequently lack a systematic feedback mechanism to tell them what they need to start doing or stop doing. Their leadership is fragile and easily shocked by unexpected information. Contrast this with those who build a personal feedback loop: their leadership is more robust as they've reduced the risk of shocks from unforeseen directions. These people are role models who believe in seeking feedback and acting upon it constructively because receiving feedback is the best way to get better at almost anything.

Here are five steps from their rule book that you can use early in your career to build a supportive, challenging feedback loop:

1. **Ask your current boss for feedback proactively.** Specificity is essential. Don't just ask, "How am I doing?" What could you be doing more of, start to do or stop doing to be more helpful/impactful in the team? Look to help solve their problems, and link the feedback to the issues they may be facing.

2. **Find a mentor at work** who will observe you in action and provide timely and constructive criticism.

3. **Ask a friend at work or someone you know outside work.** Again, be specific; vague questions yield vague answers.

4. **Ask a trusted peer to provide specific feedback**; have them observe you in specific situations – such as meetings – and offer targeted feedback.

5. **Observe successful people in action.** What do they do that makes them so successful, and how is it different to what you do? How might you develop that skill or behaviour authentically?

To paraphrase a tweet from the author Shane Parrish:

> *Don't make the mistake of asking for feedback from people who are too nice. Kind people are okay, but nice people rarely give helpful feedback. Kind people will tell you things a nice person won't. A kind person will tell you that you have spinach between your teeth. A nice person won't because it would make them uncomfortable.*[11]

A well-designed feedback loop is a system that supports a leader's development efforts. Feedback is the beginning, not the end, of a continuous learning and development process.

What's your sense of fragility or robustness in the face of feedback?

---

11. Parrish, S. [@ShaneAParrish], 2023, 27 October. *Too often, the people we ask for feedback are nice but not kind.* [Post] X. https://twitter.com/ShaneAParrish/status/1717869790230991131?s=20 [Accessed 30 October 2023]]

ALL I WANT TO KNOW IS WHERE MY CAREER GOES OFF THE RAILS, SO I'LL NEVER GO THERE

Inspired by the book entitled *All I Want To Know Is Where I'm Going To Die, So I'll Never Go There*,[12] this bonus principle invokes the power of "inversion". Despite our best intentions, thinking forward and following the 12 principles in the leadership toolkit isn't always successful. "Inversion" is a thinking process in which you consider the opposite of what you want to achieve. Instead of directly seeking success, it involves thinking about how to avoid failure, which – for some people – can lead to more effective strategies as a result of highlighting any obstacles and risks that might not be immediately apparent. By inverting, we gain new perspectives that align well with critical thinking and challenging assumptions, which are crucial to progressing along your leadership journey.

What does this mean in practice for you in your early career? Well, if you recognise yourself in the following paragraphs, it's an early warning sign that your leadership journey is at risk of derailing.

---

12 Bevelin, P., 2016. *All I Want To Know Is Where I'm Going To Die So I'll Never Go There: Buffet and Munger – a study in simplicity and uncommon, common sense.* London: Walsworth.

Being eager to make a mark, your obsession with perfection becomes a double-edged sword. Due to striving for flawlessness in every task, you often delay critical deliverables and fail to meet expectations.

Simultaneously, you neglect personal well-being. Spending long hours at the office, coupled with poor eating habits and minimal exercise, starts taking a toll. You mistake this self-neglect for dedication, not realising it's setting the stage for your future burnout.

In the whirlwind of daily tasks, you lose sight of the core purpose of the business and the needs of its clients. Through being caught up in a mire of low-priority, low-value tasks, you fail to align your efforts with the company's overarching goals, leading to a misallocation of energy and resources.

As your career progresses, you become more concerned about crafting a personal brand, and a gap emerges between your perception and reality. You focus more on how you're seen than on developing actual skills and competencies, leading to a professional persona that lacks substance.

In this quest for recognition, you start chasing superficial prestige, mistakenly equating it with genuine respect and accomplishment. This desire to impress others overshadows the importance of building a foundation of true competence and integrity.

Communication becomes another battlefield. You adopt an assertive, fast-talking style and frequently dominate conversations, leaving little room for listening or understanding alternative viewpoints. This approach alienates your colleagues and hinders collaborative efforts.

By misinterpreting the professional environment as being familial, you naïvely overlook the competitive and performance-driven nature of the workplace. You fail to recognise that, unlike with a family, a corporate team's primary goal is to deliver top-quality products or services.

Your ambition and early successes have bred a dangerous overconfidence. You start ignoring the basic principles that effected your initial wins, creating blind spots that threaten to derail and stall the career momentum you've established.

Socially, you surround yourself with colleagues who drain rather than energise you, mistaking shared grievances and water-cooler conversations for meaningful relationships. This environment of mediocrity and negativity starts dragging down your performance and outlook.

In dealings with management, you remain passive under poor leadership. You endure the realities of working for an okay manager without attempting to communicate more effectively or seek ways to improve the situation.

Attending meetings becomes another hurdle. Your frustration at poorly run meetings shows in how you engage and participate. You remove yourself from active involvement, reducing the opportunities to positively impact how you and those around you spend a significant amount of your time at work.

You fall into the trap of constant comparison with your peers. This habit fosters dissatisfaction and diverts focus from how you're uniquely positioned to make a difference. Unaware of this, you let the achievements of others overshadow the joy of your own accomplishments.

You cross one of the following three red lines:

1. You violate laws, company policies or regulations.
2. You bully or intimidate others.
3. You engage in harassment of some kind.

Crossing any of these boundaries will likely result in swift termination from your job and could severely damage your career. There are no shortcuts worth this risk; the consequences are unequivocal. In essence, you'll "Go directly to jail. Do not pass go. Do not collect £200." If you ever find yourself uncertain about the ethical implications of an action, employ this litmus test: ask yourself, "How would my parents react if they saw a headline about me doing this on the front page of a newspaper or online?"

The professional journey is fraught with challenges. Many, if not all, will encounter these pitfalls at various stages. Recognising and addressing them is key to staying on track. The following exercise will help you identify where you might be going wrong and hence where you need to prioritise making changes.

HEALTH CHECK: PERSONAL EVALUATION TOOL (PET)

The PET is designed as a health check to help you assess your current knowledge and skills, now you've read the principles.

How to complete the PET

For each of the 12 principles, think about related occasions when you're at work. Think of your typical day and week and your interactions with others – not just one good or bad example. If you have yet to start your career, think about your experience in the context of student organisations, volunteering, summer internships and other workplaces. For each principle, enter a subjective self-assessment value from 1 to 5 (as per the meanings in the following table). Your answers will create awareness and insights by painting a picture of how you view yourself. Be transparently honest with yourself. Your answers will help to clarify, define and prioritise the areas to work on. Revisit and update the PET every six months to monitor your progress and ensure you're targeting the principle that's likely to have the most impact.

Rank Description

Rank	Description
1	I need help! My actions are all over the place.
2	I need a sustained effort to implement the principles.
3	I follow the principles inconsistently, with occasional flashes of inspiration.
4	I'm getting there. More time is required to master the principles.
5	My actions consistently align with the principles.

Principle	Question	Trip Hazard	Rating (1 to 5)
#1. Grasp the table stakes: Deliver on spec, on time and on budget. Consistency, even in small actions, is key. Leave strategy to others initially.	Do you do what you say you'll do when you say you'll do it?	You allow the pursuit of perfection to get in the way of the work you need to do. Perfectionism is often a place in which to hide. Perfection can be an excuse we use as the reason not to speak up or deliver.	
#2. Invest in yourself: Say *yes* early in your career. View spending time and money on learning, tools and new habits as fuel for success.	Are you investing in yourself and creating an edge, or are you moving with the tide, comfortable doing the same thing everyone else does?	You don't look after yourself: you're lacking sleep, exercise, rest, good food and time to recharge. If you don't make time for your wellness, you'll be forced to make time for your illness.	

Principle	Question	Trip Hazard	Rating (1 to 5)
#3. Maintain focus: Avoid distractions. Staying focused on top priorities sets successful people apart.	What's your oxygen?	You forget why you're in business. Who are your clients, and what do they want? And how does your work and your team's work support that?	
#4. Craft your unique story: Understand and control your personal brand. Know what words people associate with you.	What do you want people to think of when they hear your name?	You over-focus on your personal brand, and your brand and craft become divorced. Investing in your brand takes precedence over investing in getting better at your craft.	
#5. Cultivate gravitas: Develop your presence. Gravitas can lead others to feel more confident in you, irrespective of your experience.	Who has left a lasting impression on you throughout your education or career?	You chase prestige. It's okay to want to impress other people, but choose the right people. At best, prestige is a trailing indicator. At worst, it increases the noise level and hence increases distraction.	
#6. Enhance your communication skills: Effective communication is key. Master listening, writing and public speaking.	Are you putting more energy into the room than you're taking out?	You become a fast-talking, assertive speaker as a way of pushing your agenda past other people's examination. This is at the expense of developing your listening skills as you emphasise listening to respond rather than to gain understanding.	

Principle	Question	Trip Hazard	Rating (1 to 5)
#7. Be a valued team member: Aim to be a collaborator, not just a leader. Working with others to achieve goals is vital early in your career.	How focused are you on your own goals versus the team's?	You think of the for-profit company you work for as a family, rather than as a sports team that only exists to provide a top-quality product or service to its clients.	
#8. Make better decisions: Use robust frameworks for decision-making. Recognise the trade-offs involved.	Where are you focusing your mental resources to make the most-effective decisions?	You gain early success and traction because you're ambitious and talented. Beware! Early success can make you overconfident, which will cause you to ignore or forget these core principles. This creates blind spots, and blind spots may derail your career.	
#9. Engage strategically with stakeholders: Networking isn't self-promotion; it's essential. Build relationships strategically.	What are you so busy doing that you don't have the time, energy or capacity to build relationships?	You surround yourself with people who drain your energy rather than those who energise you, or with those who are B or C players, rather than A players, which drags you down.	
#10. Master managing upwards: Communicate proactively to show control. Managing your manager shows initiative and empowerment.	What level of initiative do you feel comfortable operating at?	You endure, without attempting to improve the situation, the realities of working for a manager who doesn't want to engage or develop their direct reports.	

Principle	Question	Trip Hazard	Rating (1 to 5)
#11. Run effective meetings: Your well-run meetings can stand out amid poorly managed ones. Free up headspace and time for others.	How do you rate the meetings you attend?	You encounter people who don't want to change, which leads to frustration and resentment. Change is hard. Every change carries with it the possibility of conflict and uncertainty. Your boss, who leads many of the meetings you attend, may regard the workplace environment as dynamic and difficult enough without looking for trouble.	
#12. Seek out feedback: Maintain a feedback loop for continuous improvement, like elite sports teams do.	What's your sense of fragility or robustness in the face of feedback?	You become dissatisfied because you compare yourself to others. As you get more years under your belt, you'll come across many successful people who didn't deserve the credit they got. It doesn't matter. Play your game and focus on yourself. Comparison is the thief of joy.	

Select no more than three principles from the previous table, for which you have rated yourself as a 1 or 2, to work on. What small changes can you make to shift yourself from where you are currently to where you want to be?

CONCLUSION

Certainly, there's more to creating leadership success than the principles described in this book. There are mission statements, team culture, dealing with conflict and confronting poor performance, attracting and retaining talent, and a host of other tactical and strategic considerations. However, each element of leadership revolves around the basic principles I've shared: disciplined attention to execution; investing in continuing improvement; controlling your career story; mastering communication skills; avoiding distractions and maintaining focus; learning to make better decisions; building relationships strategically, including with your superiors; an unrelenting commitment to sound principles, such as running excellent meetings; and seeking feedback, coupled with the acceptance of what it means to be a team player.

Despite my best efforts to follow these leadership principles, I've made many mistakes over the years. I definitely wish I'd made fewer errors. But if you're growing and developing throughout your career, and especially in the early stages, the reality is that you'll make mistakes. Embrace these errors as stepping stones; each one is an opportunity for refinement and progress.

Remember, the aspiration to work under great leadership is universal. Most people want to work for amazing managers. Such managers are essential for your career, but you can't rely on the lottery of working with a really good manager early on. Later, after a few years, you can intentionally decide to move to another team or organisation, especially if you're in a career that rewards you for your judgement in making good decisions. Initially, you may start your career working for an okay or absentee manager, so you should turn yourself into someone who can do outstanding work even without a great manager. These principles will help you to achieve that.

A leadership development initiative doesn't work like a vaccine: get inoculated against doing bad things, and off you go into the future as a flexible and empowering leader of a successful team. Where behavioural change is involved, development is a long-term, ongoing process. Treat your career as a learning laboratory in which you conduct small, low-risk experiments to build the momentum that defines your career.

Finally, recognise that little in this world is achieved just from thinking and reading about ideas and concepts. True transformation stems from action. Let the exercises, such as the one on page 61, guide your initial steps towards tangible change. Now you're armed with insights and strategies, turn the page from concept to practice. It's time to act, to evolve and to excel. Get started, and let each small adjustment build the momentum that tilts the odds in your favour for career success.

WHAT'S NEXT?

Ready to elevate your leadership game? Here's your next move

Unlock exclusive insights: Subscribe to my free email newsletter on Substack at robertyeo.substack.com. Equip yourself with game-changing strategies in leadership, coaching and productivity.

Spread the wisdom: Found value in this book? Don't keep it to yourself. Share it with a colleague or friend who's as committed to excellence as you are.

Join the conversation: Let's connect! Follow me on LinkedIn at linkedin.com/in/robertyeo-rylncoaching/ for timely insights and spirited debates on leadership and coaching.

***RYse Journal*:** Elevate your self-coaching with my purposely designed notebook. Buy yours on Amazon today and start tracking your path to mastery.

Share the toolkit: Share the 12 principles that make up the leadership toolkit with your mentors, peers and friends. Don't worry about giving away any proprietary knowledge. It's a good trade. It's smart. The activity of sharing will lead to so many positive things to help you with your upward career trajectory that the negatives are minuscule in comparison.

READING, WATCHING AND LISTENING LIST

Being the best-informed person in your team requires continuous learning to be part of your daily routine.

As Richard P. Feynam says:

> Knowledge isn't free. You have to pay attention.

There really are no excuses. Fill your empty time. Make learning part of your routine when you commute, walk the dog, exercise or when you're performing manual tasks, which you can do by listening to a podcast. Here are three short lists of my recommendations.

Podcasts:

- *The Tim Ferriss Show.* Available at: https://tim.blog/podcast/
- *The Knowledge Project.* Available at: https://fs.blog/knowledge-project-podcast/
- *Founders.* Available at: https://www.founderspodcast.com/
- *All-In.* Available at: https://www.allinpodcast.co/

Email newsletters:
- Farnam Street. Subscribe here: https://fs.blog/
- Seth Godin. Subscribe here: https://seths.blog/
- Doomberg. Subscribe here: https://substack.com/@doomberg
- Paul Graham. Subscribe here: https://www.paulgraham.com/articles.html
- David Perell. Subscribe here: https://twitter.com/david_perell

Books:
- Collins, J. 2016. *Good to Great*. San Francisco, CA: Instaread.
- Covey, S.R. 1999. *The 7 Habits of Highly Effective People.* New York, NY: Simon and Schuster.
- Koch, R. 1999. *The 80/20 Principle.* Sydney: Currency.
- Goldsmith, M. 2007. *What Got You Here Won't Get You There.* London. Hachette Books.
- Eurich, T., 2018. *Insight.* London: Pan Macmillan.
- Newport, C. 2016. *Deep Work.* London: Piatkus.
- Kerr, J. 2013. *Legacy.* London: Constable.
- Gawande. A. 2011. *The Checklist Manifesto: How to get things right.* London: Profile.
- Meyer, E. 2014. *The Culture Map.* New York, NY: Public Affairs.
- Kegan, R. 2009. *Immunity to Change.* Brighton, MA: Harvard Business Review Press.

Follow the experts on LinkedIn, X/Twitter and Substack. There's an unbelievable amount of knowledge and wisdom that you can tap into for free – if you can be bothered to look.

ABOUT ME

I'm Robert Yeo, an executive coach.

My coaching is a mixture of consultation, exploration, challenge, discussion, support, experimentation and mentoring. Although they're flexible and far-reaching, the coaching conversations are situational and intentional. There are business challenges plus career and personal development agendas to satisfy.

I also write about leadership, coaching and productivity. I view writing as a process by which we improve our thinking and learning: writing is the process that helps me figure things out. And conveniently, I view *process* as crucial to my work and life more broadly. In fact, the quote attributed to the American sculptor Elizabeth King stating "It is only process that saves us from the poverty of our intentions"[13] helps me maintain my focus.

I want to teach, coach and challenge how we think about the

---

13 Ferriss, T. 2020. *The Tim Ferriss Show transcripts: Seth Godin on the game of life, the value of hacks, and overcoming anxiety (#476).* [Online] https://tim.blog/2020/10/29/seth-godin-the-practice-transcript/ [Accessed 5 June 2023]

problems we face. I have a fairly unique background: I'm a former managing director and chief operating officer in investment banking, and now I'm an executive coach. Too few people with this experience speak out and take the intellectual risk because they have no economic incentive to do so. The vast majority are too busy increasing their wealth to spend time getting into the area of ideas. Unfortunately, this means academics and think tanks that have rarely actually worked in industry or created and run businesses dominate the idea-generating forums of today.

You might ask why bother? What can you actually change?

Well, for one thing, I think I can provide insight and education by dissecting and explaining topics and by providing alternative solutions and points of view.

And second, I want to remind people of the importance of questioning what they read, hear and see – so as to think differently. When challenged with different opinions and points of view, emphasise discovery not defence.

Printed in Great Britain
by Amazon